This language notebook belongs to

____

CLASS _______________________________

TEACHER _______________________________

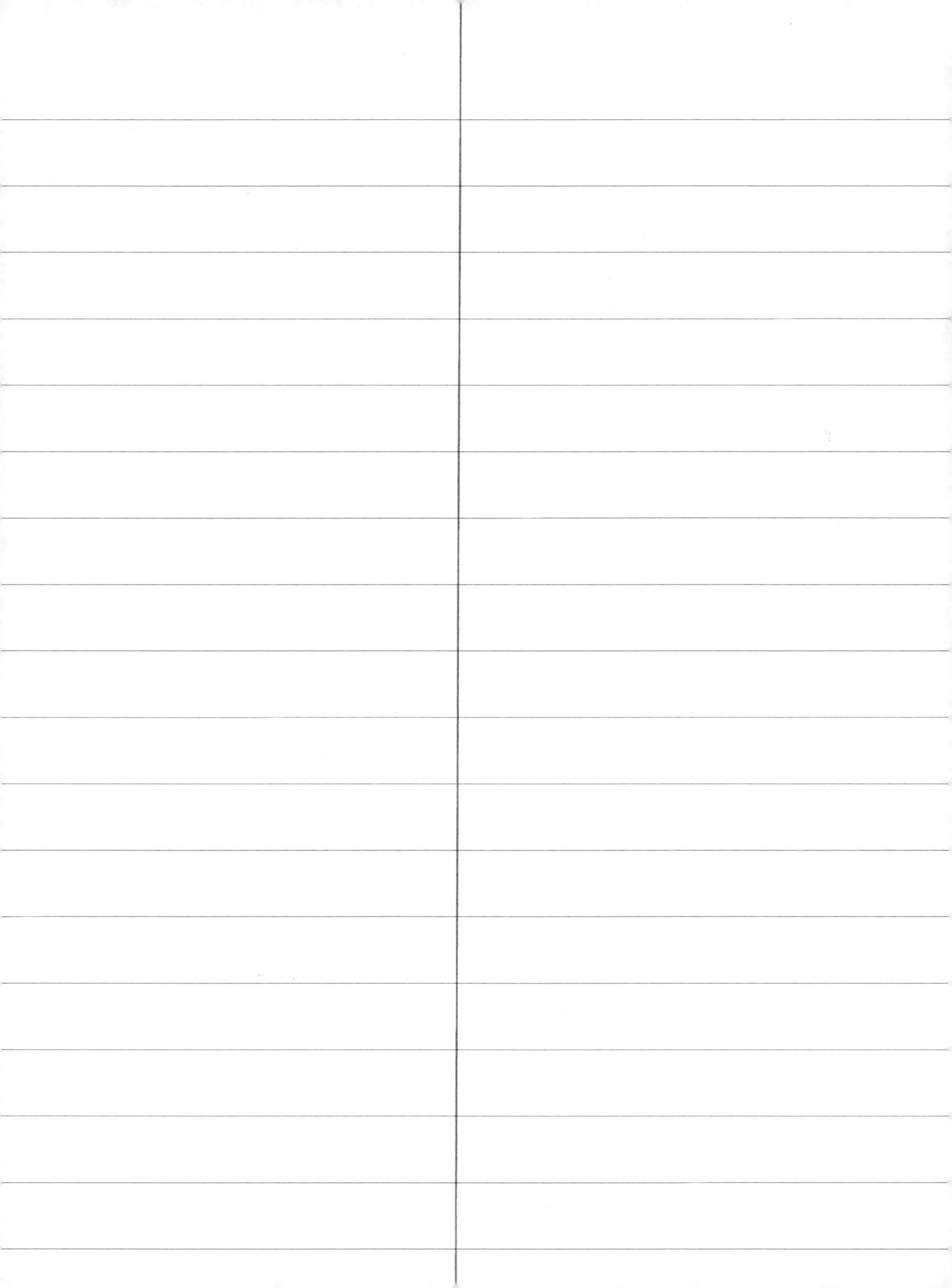

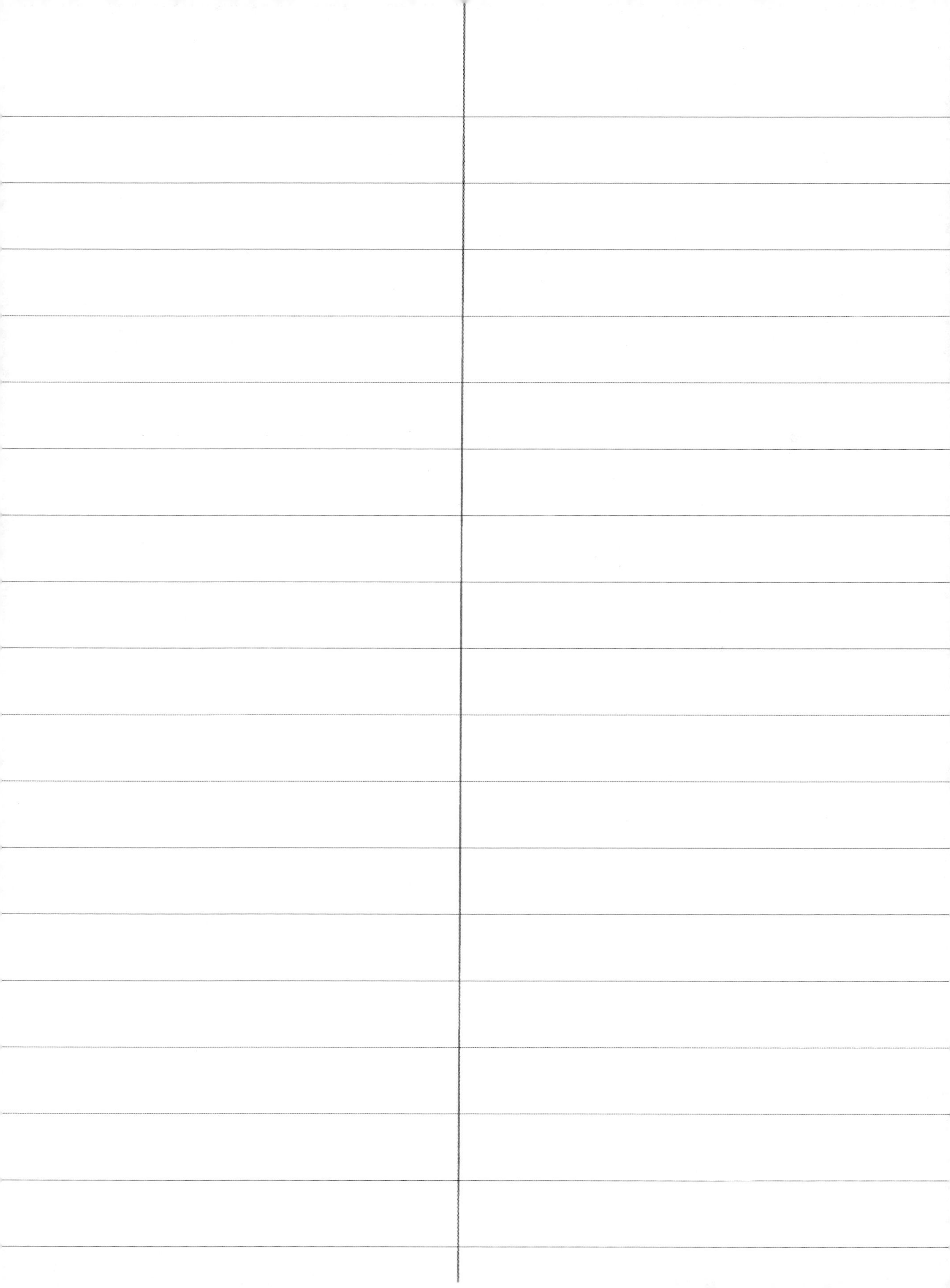

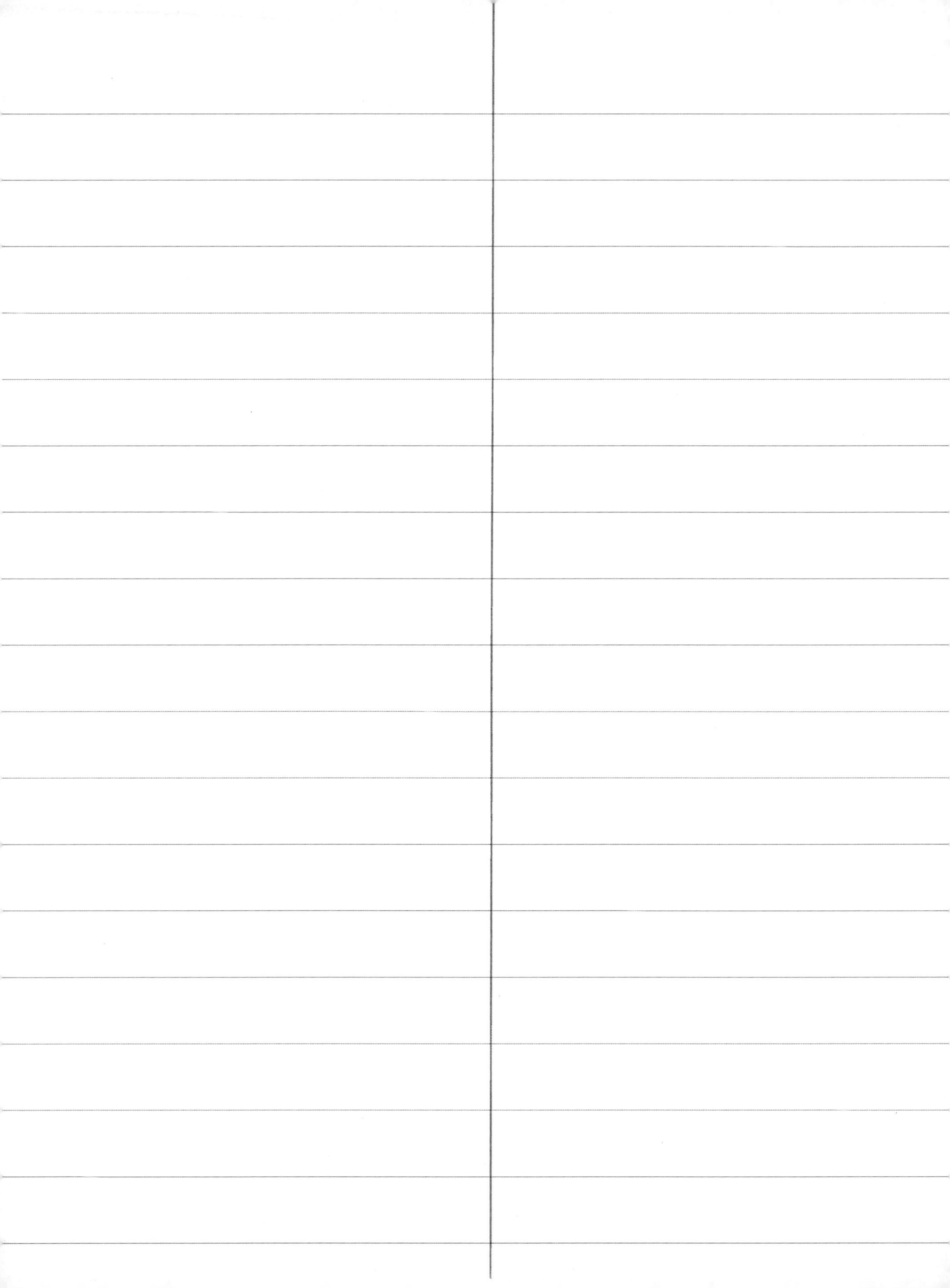

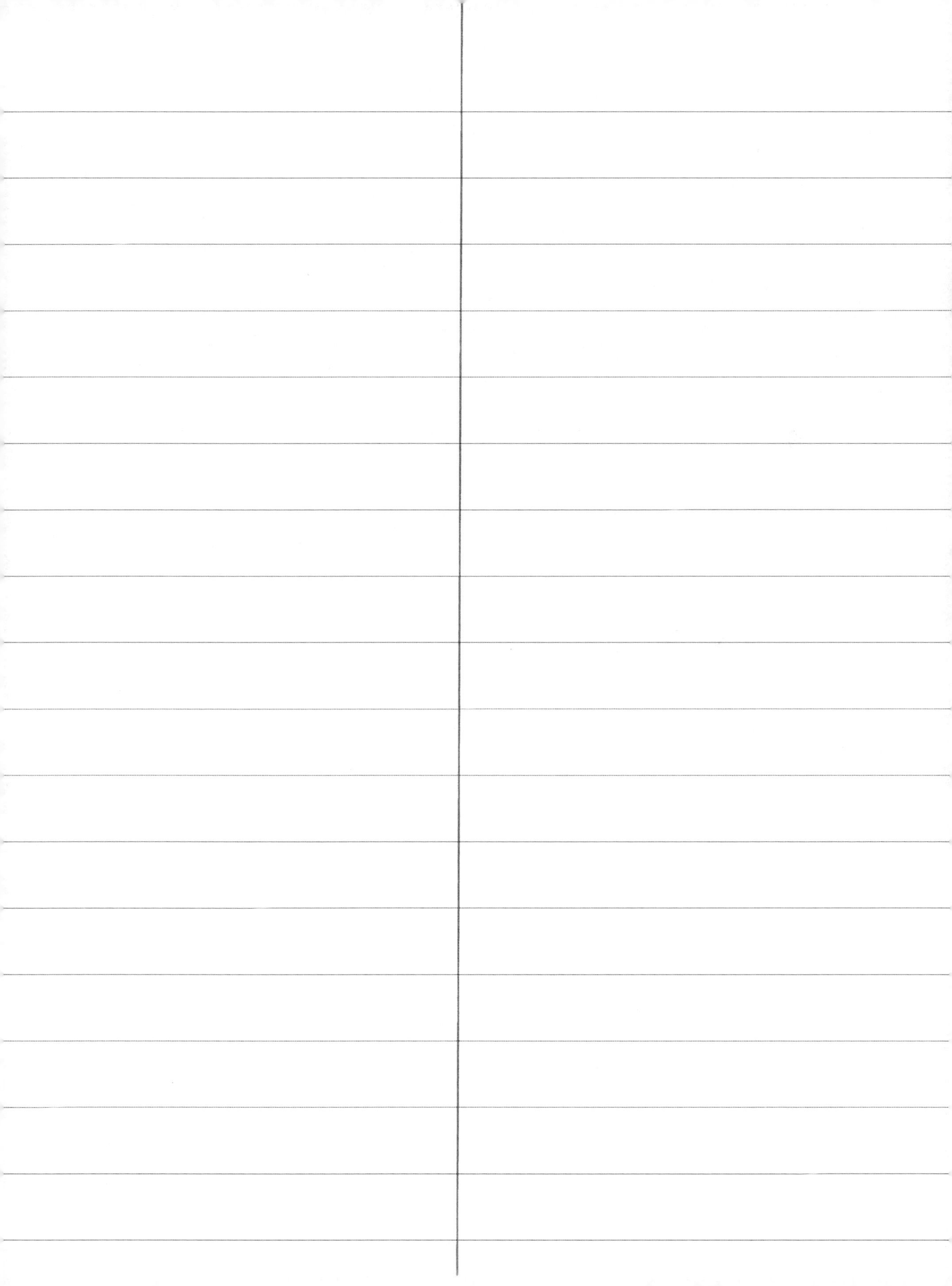

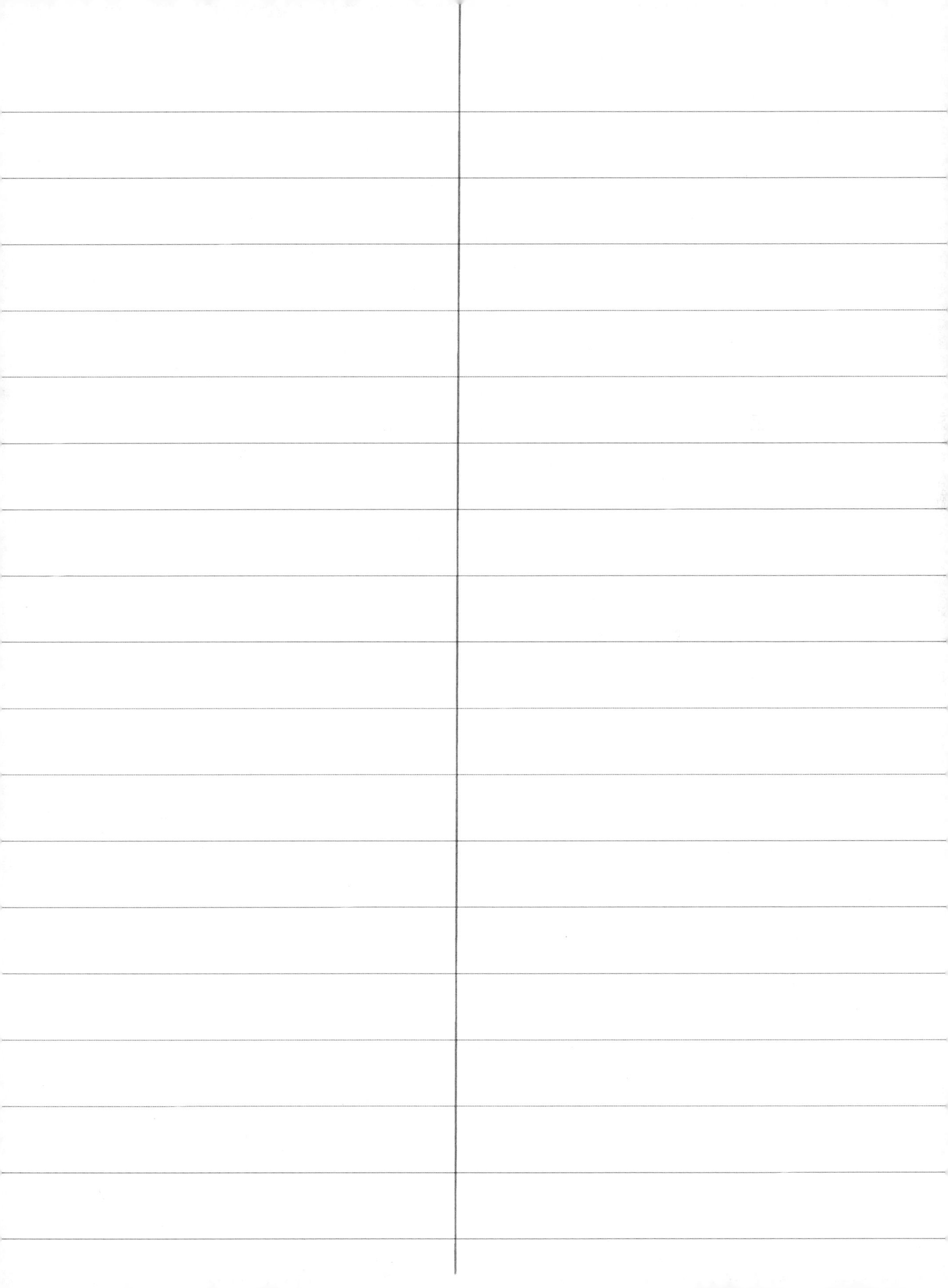

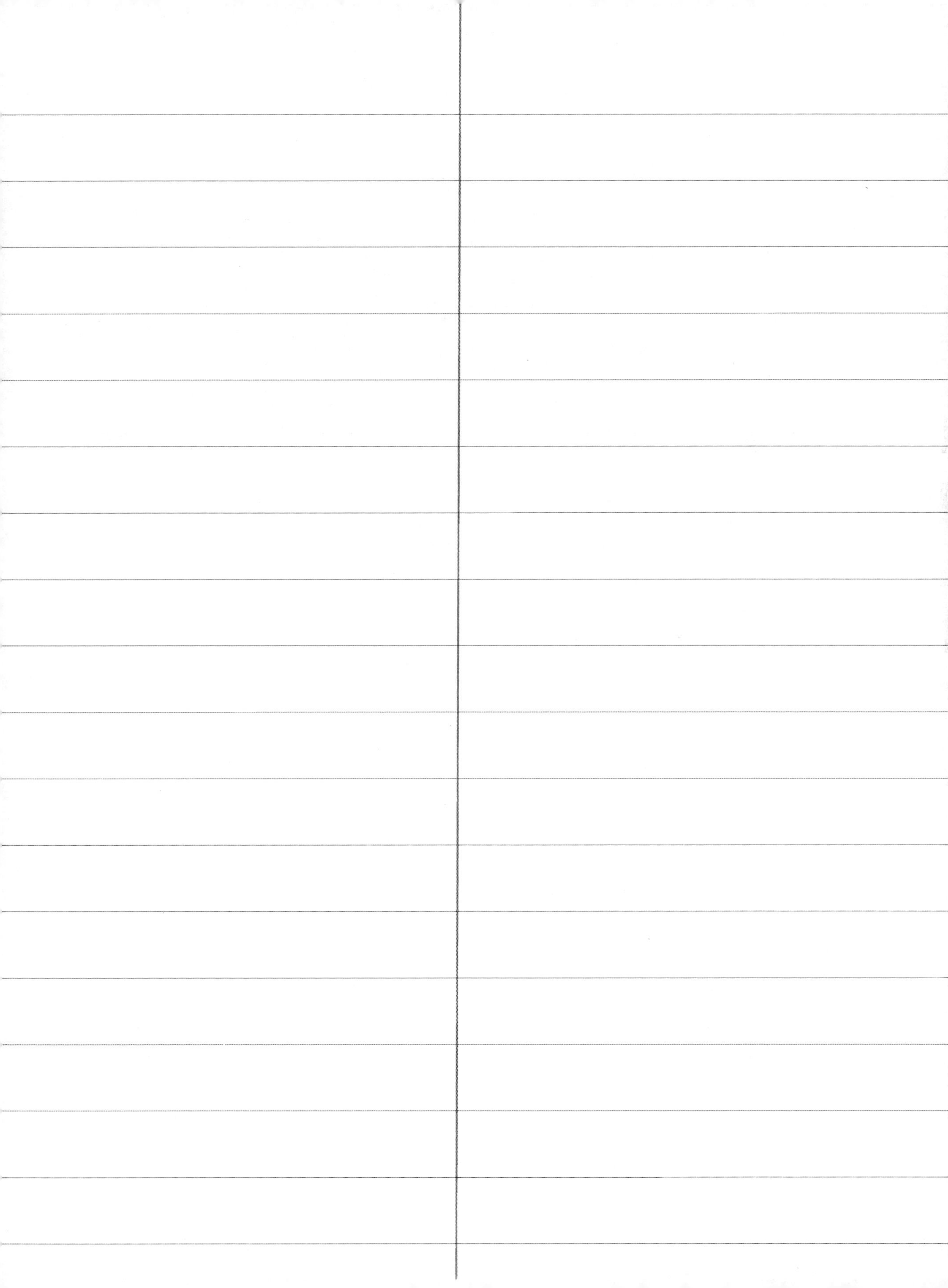

Made in the USA
Monee, IL
07 July 2026